D0645507

SEX IS NOT A FOUR LETTER Word But RELATIONSHIP Often Times Is

||||||||||||||||||||||||||||||||||||||||||||||||

by
Gary M. Douglas
and
Dr. Dain C. Heer

authorHOUSE™

1663 LIBERTY DRIVE, SUITE 200
BLOOMINGTON, INDIANA 47403
(800) 839-8640
WWW.AUTHORHOUSE.COM

First published by AuthorHouse 2/3/2006

ISBN: 1-4208-9544-3 (sc)

Printed in the United States of America
Bloomington, Indiana

This book is printed on acid-free paper.

CONTENTS
||||||||||||||||||||||||||||||||

INTRODUCTION
||||||||||||||||||||||||||||||||||||||||||||||||||||

This book about sex and relationship is an invitation to greater consciousness and greater possibilities, and offers a fresh view of how to create your relationship. We hope the things we have written will blow your mind, push you into a place of questioning, and make you say, "You're full of sh-t! How can you say that?" Everything in this book is about getting you to look at yourself and your relationship from a different place, so you can have a different possibility and a different choice.

Some of the things we talk about will contradict all of your ideas about the way things should be. We may challenge what you've been told in every class about sex and relationship you've ever taken, everything you've read about the subject, and everything you've been told by all the so-called experts. But if those things really worked, wouldn't you have been free, expansive and joyful in your relationship a long time ago? Maybe learning to question what doesn't work will open the way to find something that does. After all, if what you have been taught were working, wouldn't you have an incredible result now?

In conventional terms, success in relationship often means you get married, you have children and you keep that marriage together until death do you part. Our point of view is different. We believe the most important part of a successful relationship is to have true intimacy with yourself. If you have that, you can be alone and be happy and not judge yourself as a spinster or a weird bachelor or a gay guy. You can be by yourself and enjoy you, which is really the place everyone should be. How many people do you know who have that? Our point of view is that when you have intimacy with yourself, only then can you truly create a great relationship with another.

In this book, we discuss the five elements for creating great intimacy and offer many other points of view about sex and the nature of relationship. We hope you will use this information to create extraordinary relationships that have ongoing spark, verve and vitality and sex unlike anything you have experienced before.

So to begin, here are some questions to consider: What are the questions you need to ask to create the relationship you want? What would it take for a relationship to work for *you*—not for anyone else? What would it take for you to feel expansive in your relationship? What would it take for you to perceive the possibilities, not the limitations? What would it take for you to stop judging yourself and your mate and to recognize that you have a different choice?

IS RELATIONSHIP WHAT YOU REALLY WANT?

IIIIIIIIIIIIIIIIIIIIIIIIIIIIIIIIIIIIIIIIIIIIIIIIIIIIIIIIIIIIIIIIII

Is relationship what you really want? Personally, I'm not interested in relationship; I'm interested in consciousness. I'm interested in communion. Communion is not the wafer or the wine you take on Sunday; it is an awareness of all things. It is the oneness that we all are. When I talk about communion, I mean being in communion with all things, but most importantly being in communion with yourself and your own body. You can't begin to have a relationship with another until you are in communion with yourself, and to be in communion, you must of course, be conscious.

Does Consciousness Include Sexualness?

Consciousness and spirituality are not exclusive of one another, but neither are they the same. A lot of people *do* spirituality, but they approach it from the viewpoint, *I'm right and you're wrong.* When this happens, spirituality becomes another form of religion, and it creates separation rather than communion. The difficulty with most spiritual pursuits is that they do a hell of a lot of judging.

Consciousness, unlike this kind of spirituality, includes everything and judges nothing. Does consciousness include spirituality? Does it include sexualness? Of course it does. The problem with judging is that every judgment you make stops you from receiving anything that doesn't match it. For example, if you decide that your partner is the perfect mate, you become unwilling to see when they do something against you. The moment you judge your partner to be perfect, you stop perceiving. Can you see how this works? You decide they're perfect, and then you won't see anything else. You can't perceive or receive any other information. You won't see the ways in which they don't contribute to making your life more expansive. You won't see when they are doing something against you. You stop being present in your relationship as the all-knowing, infinite being that you truly are. You begin to eliminate *you* from the relationship.

If you are experiencing a limitation or difficulty in your life around sex or relationship or anything else, there has to be something you are unwilling to perceive. In fact, if anything in your life is not working, it's because you are unwilling to perceive, know, be or receive something. That is how our relationships become limited and unhappy. In fact, it's the only way our reality becomes limited.

When you go out into the woods and you don't have any judgment about anything there, your mind is quiet. Everything is peaceful. There is a sense of beauty. You're in total connection with everything. This space you feel in nature is the communion you have with all things, which is consciousness and oneness.

We are everything. There isn't anything that we haven't been or done in one lifetime or another. If we can claim the so-called evil side of ourselves as easily as we can claim the so-called good side, then we won't spend our time trying to judge what is right or wrong about us, and we'll move into a place of oneness and consciousness.

What we're looking for is how to get to oneness with sex, relationship and copulation. If you can do this without judgment, you have freedom, but as long as you have judgment, you have no freedom. When you suppress yourself with the judgment that you are *bad*—or anything else, you create a limitation that eventually locks you out of you.

I have a friend who did a psychology class, and the professor told the students that ninety percent of the population would rather have a bad relationship than no relationship. Rather than be alone and enjoy themselves, most people would rather have a partner they're miserable with, because that means they have *someone*.

Is that enough for you? If it is, throw this book away.

But if you would like to have something greater in your life than the bullshit most people think of as relationship, then you must begin to develop a more conscious attitude toward yourself and your body, toward sex and toward communion with others. As I said at the beginning, what we're looking for is not relationship, but communion, consciousness and oneness. If this sounds interesting to you, keep reading.

HUMAN OR HUMANOID: WHICH ARE YOU?

||||||||||||||||||||||||||||||||||||||||||||||||||||||

One of the more unexpected things we've discovered with Access is the awareness that there appear to be two species of beings on planet Earth, humans and humanoids. Humans live in judgment of everybody else and think that life just is the way it is, and nothing is ever right, so don't even bother to think about another possibility.

Humanoids, on the other hand, look for ways to make things better. If you invent things, if you search out things, if you are always looking for a better, bigger way of creating something, you are a humanoid, not a human. Humanoids are the people who create change. They create the inventions, the music and the poetry. They create all the things that come out of a lack of satisfaction with the status quo.

Humanoids Judge Themselves

One of the most important things to know about humanoids is that they sit in judgment of themselves. They think there's something wrong with themselves because they're not like everyone else around them. They ask themselves, "What's wrong with me, that I can't get it right?" They wonder why they can't get what everybody else gets and do what everybody else does. When somebody lies to them, or does something wrong to them, they twist it around and look for what they've done wrong. They make themselves wrong and the other person right.

A humanoid friend of mine had been in a relationship with a woman for a long time and one day I said to him, "She's cheating on you, Raymond. I know it. She's lying to you.

He went, "No, she's not. She wouldn't do that. She's my best friend."

I asked him, "Can you confront her with this?"

So, he called her and talked with her about what I'd said, and she got really angry with him. His response to that was to judge himself hideously for having asked her.

And how many weeks did it take before he found out it was true? Six weeks later he found out she *was* cheating on him. What made it even worse was that he had disavowed his knowing. He said it was like having a truck hit him and then back up and go forward over him again.

"This Is All There Is"

I talked to my step dad, who was very definitely human, after he had a heart attack. I said, "Dad, what was it like for you having that heart attack?" Nobody had asked him that question.

He said, "Well, I remember having the heart attack and standing outside my body looking at…." He trailed off, and then started over again.

"Well, I had the heart attack and then I saw them putting the electrodes on my chest…." Again, he stopped mid-sentence, waited a moment, and then started over again.

"Well," he finally said, "I had the heart attack and then they put the electrodes on my chest and they zapped me."

He could not have a reality in which he was out of his body watching these things occur. It was a great example of what happens to people when they can't have what doesn't fit their judgments of reality. His reality was that you are in a body and that's all there is. A human can never have anything that doesn't match the viewpoint, *This is all there is.* Humans are the people who do not believe in reincarnation. They do not believe in other possibilities. They do not believe in miracles. The doctors and the lawyers and the Indian chiefs create everything. Humans create nothing. They will do the same job over and over and over again, and sometimes very well and efficiently, but they will not ever do it differently.

Forty-seven percent of the population is humanoid and they are the creators of everything that changes in this reality. Fifty-two percent is human. (And the final one percent? Some day I'll tell you about them!) Humans hold onto things the way they are and never want anything to change. Have you ever been to somebody's house where they haven't changed the furniture in 30 years? Human.

Humans will live in the same neighborhood until the neighborhood goes downhill, and rather than moving, they will put bars over their windows to keep the *jailbirds* out of their house. And who's looking out of the bars? Excuse me, you've just made yourself into a jailbird! Humans are the contractors who tear out all of the plants so they can remodel a house. They kill everything in order to create. "That's just the way it is," they say. "We're going to kill everything and it will be fine." Humans sit in judgment of others, because everything in their life is about judgment, decisions, force and effort. It's the only place they create from.

Think of somebody you know who's human. Feel the consciousness of him or her. Now feel the consciousness of a rock. Which one is lighter? The rock? Okay. There's more consciousness in the rock, so we hang out with humans for what reason? We all have human friends and family, but they sit in judgment of us and tell us how wrong we are for everything we do.

Humans and Humanoids: Sex and Relationship

The human point of view is that sex is for procreation and you're supposed to have two children and after that you're supposed to stop having sex. The humanoid point of view is that sex is for fun. So, if you're a humanoid, you want to have sex for recreation, except that if you do that and have a good time, you might judge yourself to be bad.

Clearly, if you're a humanoid, you need a humanoid partner. But one of the greatest difficulties in creating expansive relationships is that humanoids are attracted to humans. You don't want to pick a human partner, but you may feel impelled to do that. If you do, they will live in judgment of you. They'll tell you how wrong you are about everything you do. If you're judging you and the other person is judging you, it makes it difficult for you to show up as who you are in the relationship. All the judging causes you to start divorcing you, so you can't truly be in the relationship.

Humanoids always wonder why they can't just be satisfied with things the way they are and why they can't do monogamous relationships with ease. If they "cheat" on their partner, they heap hideous amounts of judgment on themselves, whereas a human will cheat and say, "You made me do it."

"Well, If You'd Just Get a TV..."

For humanoids, it is a great relief to know that we are always judged and we never fit in. We try so hard, but we can't make ourselves fit into the human mold. Everyone in our family tells us, "Well, if you'd just get a TV, a new car and a regular job, you'd be fine."

The idea of bringing up this human/humanoid thing is not about sitting in judgment of humans. It's about becoming aware of how we humanoids judge ourselves. We look at the humans and go, "How come I can't be like them? They have it so easy." For them, life is simple because they have it categorized. Humanoids will always ask themselves, "What's wrong with me that I can't be like this other person? What's wrong with me that I can't be satisfied with less? What's wrong with me?" They go into serious amounts of judgments of themselves. All the judgments you have set in front of yourself for being humanoid, can we destroy and un-create those, please?

EMBODIMENT: WHAT IS IT?

Most spiritual teachings, most churches and religions, talk about how your body is a bad thing. They teach about the sins of the flesh and view embodiment as a negative state of affairs. But if having a body were a bad thing, why would you keep coming back? You have unlimited choice in the universe, and if you keep coming back, you must be doing it for a reason.

There has to be a greatness in embodiment that we have not yet acknowledged, which is why we keep doing it again and again, as though we think we're going to create something different. Until you see embodiment as a joyful expression of you, the infinite being, and until you can move into the greatness of what embodiment is, you cannot get free of coming back over and over again.

Watch a cat. A cat loves his body. He does back flips out of exuberance and runs for the sake of running. When he eats, he eats with relish. He doesn't eat out of obligation or because it's an opportunity to chat with somebody. He won't stop to talk with you in the middle of his dinner. Cats are in total communion with their bodies. There is no sense of separation between them and their bodies. When they walk, they use every muscle. This is the way it is with animals, but when we walk, do we use every muscle in our bodies? Or do we walk, like most people, from our knees down, like little windup toys? What do you think it would it be like if we didn't have a sense of separation from our bodies?

I have a friend who told me he isn't very athletic and that he doesn't do sports, but I have watched him run. When he comes back from his run, his arms are twice the size they were when he left, but not from doing push-ups or working those particular muscles. It's because his body loves to move. When he runs, he runs, not in the stilted, jointed "I'm jogging for my health," posture, but from the sheer delight of movement. His whole body moves when he runs. For him, life is exuberant when he has the joy of moving his body. Unfortunately, most of us never experience joy in the movement of our bodies. We push our bodies to exercise or we force them to go to the gym. We never ask them what they want to eat or what would make them feel great.

I have another friend who can have sex all night long and work all day, have sex the next night, all night long, and work the next day, and have maybe four hours of sleep the entire time. He never loses any energy. His body is a joy to him. He is one of the few people I've ever met who takes such delight in his body. Most people who have sex all night long are tired the next day and want to sleep. Not him. He is all the more enthusiastic and ready to do more. If we look at this as the real possibility, what can we create with our bodies?

I worked with a lady who came to me about weight problems. I told her, "Talk to your body about what makes it feel good and do something that nurtures your body every day."

She remembered that when she was a kid, her mother used to powder her every night after her bath. She went out and bought some scented powder and began to diligently powder her body every night. It made it feel all soft and lovely. Her body felt nurtured, cared for and honored, and she lost 25 pounds in six weeks.

I want to encourage you to experience the greatness of embodiment. It's about learning how to honor your body and care for it and recognize that it wants to serve you. It wants to make your life great.

The viewpoint isn't that you're in charge of your body and so you kick it around. No. Your body will do anything you want. All you have to do is ask. But if you look at it in the mirror and judge how fat it is, and how ugly it is, and how saggy it is, that's what you'll get more of. If you stand in front of the mirror and pet your body and tell it how cool it is, it's amazing what it will come up with. We ought to be here with this body, but most of us never even ask our bodies what they would like.

What if we could unlock whatever it is that keeps us from having the joy of embodiment? What if we could have a communion with our body and actually love our body and enjoy it? What if we could have the full exuberance of our body and be willing to feel every part of it? What if we could live our lives as the orgasmic quality life can be? Maybe a different reality could show up here on planet Earth.

WHAT DEFINES SEX?
IIIIIIIIIIIIIIIIIIIIIIIIIIIIIIIIIIIIIIIIIIIIIIIIIIIIIIIIIIIIIIIIIIII

The five elements of sex are sensuality, sex, copulation, sexualness and sexuality.

Sensuality has to do with what the body likes. It's the sensation of being caressed. It's the feeling of sun on your skin or sliding into a cozy bed. It's the smell of your favorite flower or the feeling of being held gently by someone who cares for you.

Sex is when you feel good and you look good. You're walking tall and strutting your stuff, and everybody knows it.

Copulation is when you put the bodies together.

Sexualness is the creative energy of life on planet Earth. It exists in everything. Sexualness is receiving upon this planet. It's the way in which we have communion with all things. We receive from everything, everywhere without judgment. That's the whole idea.

With sexuality, on the other hand, there is always a judgment, because sexuality refers you to a norm, which then becomes a source of division and separation. With sexuality you get judgments and methods for destroying you and your life and your reality.

For example, I want to be able to appreciate my male friend's sexualness as well as a woman's, a cat's or a tree's. But with sexuality, instead of embracing the sexualness in everyone, we think, "It's not appropriate for me to see the sexual energy in my daughter, because that means I'm having bad thoughts." No. You'd better be able to see what your daughter is going to do, or else she'll be doing it when you don't want her to. You'd better be willing to acknowledge what's going on. You've got to be able to see the gift that each person is and not make judgments about sexuality.

I once worked with a man who has a clothing store in the gay section of town. He was having trouble with his business and he asked me to help him sort out what the problem was. We examined everything, and it all looked pretty good, and then I asked him about his customers. He said, "Well, they're mostly pretty nice, but I just hate it when *those people* come in."

I asked, "Who are *those people*?"

He said, "You know, the swishy gay guys."

I asked, "Why do you hate it when they come in?"

He said, "Because they hit on me."

I said, "Okay, so when you're out in public, do you flirt with women?"

He said, "Not when my wife is around."

I said, "Okay, but you still flirt, right? Does that mean you plan to go to bed with those people?"

He said, "Well, no. I would never cheat on my wife."

I said, "These guys are flirting with you, but you won't receive their energy. If you can't receive their energy, you can't receive their money. You're turning them away from your store. You have to be willing to receive their energy and return it. You need to learn how to flirt with them. It doesn't mean you have to go to bed with them! That's not what I'm talking about."

People misidentify sexualness and think it means copulation. Well, I don't copulate with cats, but I do receive their sexualness. It's important to recognize that because you can have the sexualness of someone, it doesn't mean you have to go to bed with them.

When you are oneness with all things, you are total sexualness and there is no judgment. You are willing to receive everything on the planet. But as soon as you say, "I am this," you create a limitation. When you go into sexuality and you say, "I'm a straight male," then you can't receive energy from homosexual males and you cut off your ability to receive from everything else. That's it. You won't receive energy from plants, you won't receive energy from animals.

And you especially won't receive energy from people of the same sex.

Think about it for a moment. If you're a man and you aren't willing to have the sexualness of another man, how can you have all of what *you* are? When we refuse to receive the energy or sexualness of people of the same sex, we are refusing to have our own sexualness, as well.

If you do, "I'm a straight male," then you go into judgment of women who are gay because they might hit on your girlfriend. You try to divide the world up and make lesbians go away from your life so they won't flirt with your girlfriend. We try to cut off what we allow our girlfriend to receive and what we will let ourselves receive, and we start dividing ourselves into forms of separation called sexuality.

If you live from a place of sexualness and no judgment, you have freedom. And you can receive the entirety of the world. You can have everything you've always wanted. That's what we're shooting for: claiming and owning the totality of your sexualness and living it, instead of thinking about it as something outside of you, or something you did in the past, or something that you have to control, or something you would like to do in the future. You have it right now. It's all here.

DOES SEX HAVE MEANING?

Some people think sex has to have meaning. It does. It's called fun. Sex is a joyful expression of life. But when you try to make it *meaningful,* you go into a judgment and as soon as you go into a judgment, you are limiting what you can experience.

Once you start doing judgments, you stop being present. What do judgments look like? "Is she the one for me?" "I wonder what having babies with him would be like." "She's got such a great job. She'd make a wonderful relationship." As soon as you start creating meaning and judgments about what the other person is going to be to you, or what the significance of sex is, you're no longer present. Judgment kills every possibility. It's the nail in your coffin.

Copulation should be a joyful expression of life, and when it's done from that point of view, it's expansive and the intensity, volume and possibilities of it can increase. But when you do copulation from the viewpoint that it has meaning, you diminish energetically what is available. The significance you put on it creates a limitation and what you do is no longer expressed as unlimited space or possibility.

For example, if someone is judging, "This is the man for me," in the back of her head, she is thinking, "Well, if I'm going to have babies with him, we definitely can't have oral sex. We definitely can't have anal sex. We definitely can't have a threesome because then he won't want to marry me." She stops her behavior based on potential future judgments that her partner *might* have. She cuts out toys and different positions because she judges that her partner might judge her as not being *right* in the future. She cuts off who she is, to try to fit the projection she *thinks* will occur in the future.

You start limiting what you can have in the area of copulation and sexualness based on your judgments. Many people I've talked to about their sex lives tell me that once they have children, they stop doing anything except the missionary position. When I ask them why, they say, "Well, we're concerned about the children finding out." Excuse me, but the children are sitting outside of their bodies watching you have sex! Don't you know that? You're going to teach them that this is all they get?

I know many people who stop their behavior based on the potential future judgments that someone else might have. If this doesn't make your head twist, think about the last relationship you were in when you twisted your head to try to make yourself fit into something you weren't really capable of. I've watched all kinds of people do this, and I've done it myself. I tried to twist me in order to fit my idea of someone else's point of view. That works, based on what? When you do that, who have you just divorced? You.

In Access seminars I talk about the one, two, three of sex: The first time is for fun, the second time you're in a relationship, the third time you're on your way to the altar. A friend of mine thought I was full of shit when I said that. He decided he would test it out, and he came back to me and said, "You were right!"

He told me that he didn't think it was true for him because he was very up front about these things. He said he was very clear with the next person he copulated with. He told her, "I'd love to have sex with you, but I'm not interested in having a relationship. It'll be expansive and fun if you're willing to go there," and she said, "Absolutely, I'm not interested in a relationship, either."

So they had sex the first time and he said it was awesome. The second time, she wanted to spend the night. By the time they woke up the next morning, he said the *glomb* had begun, even though they had both said they didn't want a relationship. Not to mention that she *marked* the area with some telltale signs that she had been there: she left behind her earrings and a pair of panties in the bed. They continued to have sex with one another for a while and agreed they would have sex with other people, as well, and it was expansive and fun until she found out he had copulated with someone else. She wanted to kill him. And, he said, the same thing happened with the next ten women that he had sex with.

Men do the one, two, three of sex, as well as women. After I divorced my first wife, I remember standing in the shower the morning after I had sex with a woman for the first time. I found myself thinking, "I wonder if she's the one."

Is she's the one? I don't even know her last name and I'm wondering if she's the one! I thought, "I can't believe this! I just got out of a marriage. I don't want to get into another one."

We go into these things automatically because we're programmed to move into that space. It's what everybody does. The first time you're not trying to own the person. You're just having fun. The second time you start attaching meaning to what you are doing. You begin to create the reality you've judged you should be creating if you have sex. Well, your parents told you, "Don't be having sex unless you're in a relationship." "Don't sleep with her unless you're going to marry her." The significance you put on it creates a limitation and what you do is no longer expressed as the unlimited quality of sexualness.

What you're looking for is an ever-expanding sex life, not diminishing returns. A judgment is always required in order to make something *meaningful*, and so whenever you begin to make anything meaningful, you start diminishing returns.

What does sex as a joyful expression of life look like? Remember what the last orgasm you had was like, even if it was 100 years ago. Pull that energy through your feet and up out the top of your head. How does your body feel when you do that? More vibrant? More alive? If you keep that orgasmic quality going on, you become an invitation to your partner to desire more sex. His or her body wants that same vibration. All you've got to do is keep pulling that energy through your body.

What we are looking for is a sense of the orgasmic capacity of life and the celebration life should really be. Do you have the judgment that sex is too serious to have fun with? That you can't laugh during orgasm? That you can't give her so many orgasms that she laughs hysterically because she can't take the intensity of it anymore?

Have you ever had a relationship where you could cuddle like puppies? You just sort of roll on each other and enjoy touching each other's bodies? You're not trying to get anything. You're not trying to do anything. You are just being there comfortably, allowing your bodies to intertwine. That sense of being like puppies is a place where you start to play with your body and play with the other person's body instead of doing it from *serious*. This body was made to have fun with.

The point of view is: *That looks like fun. What else can you do? What else is possible?* I hope you will have a little bit of that curiosity and you will allow a sense of fun and aliveness to venture into other parts of your life as well.

WHAT CREATES YOUR SEXUAL ENERGY?
||||||||||||||||||||||||||||||||||||||||||||||||||||||||

What creates your sexual energy? Is it someone's attraction to you, or your hormones, or what you decide to create in your own head?

Is it you that gets turned on, or your body? What do you do to turn your body on? Or do you turn it off? Do you have all the knobs turned down to the smallest possible denominator? Have you ever kept your sexual energy turned off so it wouldn't get out of control? Have you ever thought, *I don't care how much fun I had in the past. I'll remember how cool it was, but I will never ever let it be that intense again.*

If you are in the infiniteness of your beingness, then you are total sexualness all the time. The human point of view is that you have to turn your sexualness on and off. *Oh, that girl turns me on. That guy turns me on.* Excuse me? Why aren't you turned on all the time? When I asked you to pull the energy of orgasm through your feet and up out the top of your head, your body felt great, right? Why don't you do that all the time? The reason you might not let that happen is because if you do, you have to be willing to be seen for who you really are.

Have you ever noticed people who dress sexy—except there's not an ounce of sexualness about them? They're creating an image of what they think is sexual, but they're not creating sexualness. And have you ever seen someone walking down the street dressed in grubby clothes and you think, *Oh, that girl's sexy. That guy's sexy.* Why? Because they are embodying their sexualness. They're not putting it on. It's not an image they're creating. It's the reality of who they are. Sexualness doesn't have anything to do with what you look like. It's who you are.

I have a friend who thinks and feels sexualness all the time and she is copulating constantly. She has small breasts, a rather large tushie, a pooched out stomach, and bad hair. She is not a beautiful girl, but when she walks down the street, people fall over on her. There is nothing about her body parts that is beautiful, but her beingness, and her sexualness, and her presence as herself is attractive to everyone and people are always hitting on her. Sexualness is not about the body parts; it's about what you have inside.

When you embody the totality of your sexualness, you embody the capacity to receive from anybody. It doesn't matter who looks at you or thinks you're great. But what often happens is we suppress our sexualness because we think it's bad to be that way. Suppression is the way we dominate, manipulate and control ourselves. When you do not embody the greatness of you and are not willing to receive it, when you do not pull energy into you, when you are not being the orgasmic quality of life, people go away. You're contracting and compressing yourself and denying the totality of who you are. Otherwise, people are attracted to you. They come to you at all times.

You want to be able to experience all things with ease and joy and glory. It's not about suppressing any part of you. If you want to receive abundantly in your life, you have to be willing to receive anything, whether it's money or sexualness.

THE SIMULTANIETY OF GIFTING-AND-RECEIVING

OR

GIVE-AND-TAKE?
||||||||||||||||||||||||||||||||||||||||||||||||||||||||||||

This world is pretty much based on the practice of give-and-take. It's a point of view that says, *I give you this; you give me that. If I go down on you, then you you've got to go down on me.* It's an exchange modality we're all stuck in. Gifting, on the other hand, is the ability to give to someone, and in the giving, you receive equally. With gifting, there is no separate exchange that occurs. The gift is the receiving, and the receiving is the gifting, all at the same time. When you have that, you have the elements that allow you to truly have a sense of communion with all things.

Come out of the idea of the exchange of energies, and realize that all energy is expansive. It is a different way of looking at what you are giving to someone. You are gifting to them—and in so doing, you receive simultaneously.

When you have a flowerbed full of beautiful flowers, they gift to you their fragrance and their beauty and they ask nothing in return. What they receive from you is the energy you give them and the gratitude you have for how beautiful they are.

When you go out in nature, does it gift to you? Does it expect anything in return? Nature gifts everything it has at all times and as a result it receives from everything. The fruit trees create the fruit and gift to you totally. Do they hold any of it back?

Have you ever promised your partner something in order to get what you want? This is a foolish point of view. It puts you in a give-and-take position where you're giving in order to get. You're not gifting to the person because gifting is an honoring of yourself. You're trading. You're putting a price on it. You keep doing that as though it's going to get a result, but it doesn't work because people aren't willing to trade themselves. Even prostitutes are not willing to trade themselves. They, too, wish to be honored.

Most of us get into the give-and-take process. It's not: *I'm going down on you because I love the taste and I love the smell and I love every part of it, and gee, isn't this fun and how do I get more?* It's not: *This is so much fun for me that I receive in the process,* but that is what it can be.

Part of the difficulty in relationships is that so much of them are about, *If I do this for you, you're going to do that for me. If I give this, you'll give that. If I give, then I get.* You're trading off. When you give-and-take, it creates obligation. It does not honor the simultaneity of gifting and receiving; it is not the way to create the communion that is really possible.

In the give-and-take universe you think that if you give enough, the other person will give back to you. No. If you are gifting, you don't care whether they ever give you anything in return. When you gift, you open up to receiving from everything in the universe, not just the person you're with. When you do give-and-take, you're looking for that person to return the energy you've given, which is a small flow compared to the expansive flow that is possible. When you gift in totality, you open yourself to receive the entirety of the universe and the infinite intensity of sexualness becomes possible.

You have to be willing to receive from the entirety of the universe. This is the way it works. If you do the give-and-take, it's exchange. Do you want to exchange bodily fluids or do you want to gift the person because you care about them?

COMMUNION OR RELATIONSHIP?

Sometimes people say to me, "I'm ready for communion with someone." As soon as I hear them say "with someone," I know they are doing relationship even if they are pretending they are doing communion. Don't fool yourself into thinking that you are doing communion, because communion is not with *someone*. Communion is with *everything*. When you are able to have communion with everything, then you can receive everything. It will affect not only your sex life and your relationships, it will also reflect in your money and every other part of life, as well because it's about the ability to receive.

In relationship, on the other hand, everything is an asset or a liability. It's about the state of your bank balance within your relationship. You're banking on your relationship. You think the whole thing's an asset and then you find out the whole thing's a liability. Then it's over. Recognize there is a different place to function from. It's called communion.

I have a runaway horse that won't obey anyone, ever. Obedience is not part of what he does. Dain is not an experienced rider, but he really wanted to ride that horse and kept asking me until finally I succumbed and let him. The horse took one look at Dain and went, "You're mine!" Even though he won't obey even the most expert rider, he will do anything Dain asks him to do, because he and Dain have a communion, a connection that defies the laws of this reality, which would be, "I'm the owner; you do what I want."

24

Dain can ride this horse with a halter. Nobody else in the world would dare ride him with a halter. The horse has been showing Dain how to jump, and Dain can now do things with him that caused someone who has ridden for ten years to say, "I can't believe you got your horse to do that." Dain's reply was, "I didn't *get* my horse to do that. I asked him and he did it."

Many people are willing to have that kind of communion with an animal, but they're not willing to have it with their partner. They're not willing to know what their partner truly desires. They want to be told. "Tell me what you want," they say.

And their partner says, "I can't believe I have to tell you what I want you to do." Huh? Being in communion would allow them to actually express what is possible. If you are in communion and verbal communication is required, you'll not only know it, but you'll be willing to have it. You'll be willing to ask for what you like: "Oh, that feels really good. Can you do just a little bit more of that? Just a little lower, please." Ask and you shall receive.

ARE YOU REALLY WILLING TO RECEIVE?

Most of us have receiving down to "I eat, I drink, I take a shower, I change my clothes, and I buy things." That's receiving for most people on this planet. Most of it has to do with the give-and-take of reality rather than gifting-and-receiving.

Are you someone who tends to work hard to get the result? Do you work a little too hard at things? When you do that, you're not willing to receive. You're only willing to give. You give and give and give with the idea that somehow, some of it is going to come back. Or are you someone who is unwilling to receive because you think it means you'll have to give something back? You won't let anything come in because you don't want anything to go out.

Learning to receive is the greatest thing you can do. The limitation of money, the limitation of sex, the limitation of relationship, is based on what you are unwilling to receive. The freer we are in what we can have, the more we can receive. That's the biggest limitation I see in people's lives. They will not receive certain things.

If you want to find out how to increase your ability to receive, go downtown window shopping. Look at all the things in all the windows. Every time you look at something and think, "I hate that," or "I don't like that," destroy and uncreate every decision you've made that creates that point of view. Just say to yourself or out loud, "I destroy everything that creates that point of view."

Once you can look at anything and go, "Oh! That's interesting," "That's pretty," "That's unusual," "That's different," then you can start to receive everything. You don't have a fixed point of view about what something has to look like, and something totally different can come into your life. (By the way, that doesn't mean you have to buy all the ugly stuff you see.)

I used to step in dog shit all the time. I used to have it on my shoes and it would make me crazy because I couldn't stand the smell of it. I finally went, "Okay, I've got to get over this stuff about dog shit. I've got to be able to receive dog shit." I started doing an Access process called Points of Creation to get over dog shit as an issue.

Then one day I got out of the car, and I heard," Watch Out!" When I looked down, I saw I was about to step in a pile of dog shit. I walked about three paces further and I heard, "I'm here!" and there was another pile. Now, you never see piles of dog shit within three feet of each other, especially in Santa Barbara, and ever since then, dog shit tells me it's there. I never step in it anymore. Now I don't care about it.

Dain told me about a time he was running on a trail in the mountains above Santa Barbara. He started thinking, "Gee, they've got some big snakes out here. I wonder what would happen if I got bitten by a rattle snake." A mile and a quarter into his run, he went to jump over a little stream and while he was in midair, he saw a diamondback rattler on the other side in the middle of the trail, just staring at him. Somehow, from midair, he turned around and went back to the other side. He stood there and looked at the snake. It was the most beautiful diamondback rattler he'd ever seen. The snake sat there and looked at him, and Dain got it: "Oh, you were letting me know you were here, weren't you?

He was willing to receive the information that there was a snake on the trail, but he wasn't willing to recognize what it meant. The information is there—if we are willing to receive it. That's where the question, "What's right about this I'm not getting?" comes in. In Dain's case, it was, "Oh, Okay. Is there a snake out there in front of me?" Yeah. "All right, then, I'll be a little more careful."

Often in a relationship, when you aren't willing to see the rattlesnake, you make a decision, "Oh! She's the most beautiful woman in the world." You've already decided that she's beautiful, and you will not see where she's doing mean things. You will not see where she's doing ugly shit. You will not see. You've made your decision. You've made your choice and you ain't going to see anything else.

You're going to get a negative result because you aren't willing to receive everything. If you're willing to receive that there's good, bad and ugly in every person, then you can look at what they do and you can have total trust in them. You'll know they're going to eat your heart out. You'll know that they'll screw you for a nickel. You'll know what they're going to do and there's no surprise. That's where people foul up in their relationships. They decide someone is perfect and they try to see only the good. Can you see what someone is doing when you're not willing to see everything about him or her? If you're not willing to receive their limitations, are you really willing to have a relationship with them? You've made a decision and you've made a judgment and when you do that, nothing that doesn't fit that judgment comes into your awareness.

BODY, WHERE DO YOU WANT TO BE TOUCHED?

||||||||||||||||||||||||||||||||||||||||||||||||||||||||||||||||||||||||||||||||

One of the ways you can develop your awareness of what your partner's body wants is to ask his or her body what it would like and follow whatever it tells you. You don't have to ask out loud, although you can; you can also do it in your head. Start from the point of view that if you ask the body where it wants to be touched, it will tell you where to put your hands. You simply ask your partner's body what it wants, and trust that your hands will respond.

This prepares you for the most important part of great copulation, which is following the energy. Like anything else, it just takes practice. You simply ask the other person's body, "Body, where would you like to be touched? Body, what do you need?" and know that your hands will automatically go there. The back may need a lot of deep massage to release whatever tension has been created. The feet may want to be massaged, or the belly may want to be rubbed gently for a long time.

Whatever you're doing is about healing, and you have that awareness as you touch the other person's body. Healing is part of the reality of true sexualness. Your body will be trying to heal your partner's body. And their body will then try to heal yours, and that will expand both of you. It's not really anything more than asking the body, "Body, where would you like me to touch?"

Have you ever had a massage from somebody who pushed too hard, and it didn't feel good? They weren't talking to your body and letting it tell them what it wished to receive. When somebody actually talks to your body, they touch it just right. That's exactly what you want with sex: someone touches your body and they touch it just right. Sexualness is healing, it's caring, it's nurturing, it's creative, it's expansive. It heals you and your partner.

If you talk to your partner's body while you're having sex, their body will tell you what you need to do. It will tell you how slow or how fast to move. Always be willing to slow down. Intensity increases with slowness and gentleness, not with rapidity, force and friction. The slower you go, the more intense it becomes, because the other person begins to anticipate.

Great, expansive sexualness is about asking the body what it wants and following the energy. It's not about the friction, it's not about the force, it's not about the violence. And it's not about the techniques you use. Some people are into using techniques such as those taught by practitioners of Tantric sex, but we've found this is actually a limited perspective because it promotes the use of techniques, rather than awareness.

If you are following the energy, you will know exactly where to touch someone. With techniques, sex becomes a doingness, but you want it to come from your beingness. Sexualness is always a beingness. It's part of who we are. If you want to be good in bed, start asking your parnter's body what it wants, and create it with slowness and gentleness.

Following the energy is an ongoing process. You continue to be aware. You touch the body where it asks to be touched, and you notice a difference in the energy, and then you ask, "Okay, what else would you like me to do? What else is possible?" You recognize that the entire body is a sexual organ, and you are in a constant state of motion and awareness of what it is asking for and how it responds to what you do.

What some people tend to do is ask the body what it desires and focus on that one point. "Okay," they think, "I'll put my attention on the breasts, and that's all I need to do." But the truth is that making the breasts a focal point of your attention may not be what the body desires. You need to continuously receive the information that the body is giving and continuously gift to the person you're with. Even while you're touching the body in response to its request, you are aware of what is occurring for it as a result of your touch, and tuning in to what it wants next. We call this process of continuous awareness *remaining in the question.*

Later on we're going to explain how to give your partner, male or female, a full body orgasm. We hope you will learn how to ask your partner's body what it wants and trust your body to respond to its request, because that is how you begin to get there. The important thing is to practice, practice, practice, as often as you can.

BODY, WHO SHOULD I SLEEP WITH?

How many times have you decided to have sex with someone based on the size and shape of their body parts, rather than on what your body desires? If we ask our bodies to show us who to sleep with, they will tell us what's best for them. When you let your body tell you who is going to be nurturing to it and what kind of energy is going to feel good to it, then you'll be able to expand what you achieve with your body. Otherwise, sex becomes a limitation. You get into force and violence with sex because you're trying to override what your body knows is good for it.

Start talking to your body and ask it to show you who to sleep with. I had asked this question of my body, and one Sunday in Santa Barbara, when I was walking around at a swap meet, I felt a tug at my body and turned around and there was the ugliest woman I'd ever seen in my life. "Oh great," I thought, "I have to sleep with her?" I walked on and I felt another tug and looked over, and there was a gay guy and I went, "Oh now, I'm gay and I like ugly people." I walked on a little further and I felt another tug and I looked over and there was an old lady in a walker and I thought, "Ugly, gay, geriatrics. My options are fading fast." As I continued to walk, I felt another tug and there was a ten-year old boy, and I thought, "Now I'm a pedophile. Body, what are you trying to tell me?"

All of a sudden I got it. It was the energy that those people had in common. All of those people had a certain energy that was nurturing to my body. I had never asked my body what nurtured it or what would be wonderful for it with regards to sex. I'd always assumed the point of view, "Okay, I want that beautiful one over there with the amazing body." I had all those criteria of what was great, but I had never asked my body what it desired.

This is something that most of us do. We invalidate our body's choices. But if you let your body tell you what is going to be nurturing to it and what kind of energy is going to feel good to it, then you'll be able to expand what you achieve with your body. I've watched many of my friends choose women who are totally wrong for them every time. I look at them and go, "This woman is going to eat you." And they say, "No, she's good, she's wonderful, she's everything I've ever wanted." Five weeks later, "She's a stalker. I can't get rid of her. She's crazy. She's a loon. Why do I always pick women like this?" And they keep picking the same woman over and over again in a different body.

Start talking to your body and ask it to show you who would nurture it. If you end up feeling that the married man down the street is the one who is going to nurture you, recognize that somebody else has really done well. It's not about having that person. It's about the kind of energy you need to look for if you're really going to create an extraordinary, wonderful, expansive relationship.

HOW DOES HE (OR SHE) TOUCH THINGS?

For great sex, you want a partner who is sensual. If you're interested in a woman, watch how she touches things. Somebody who caresses everything in her life will caress you, too. Someone who slams things down and moves them quickly will use you the same way. A woman who leads when you dance will also slam you.

A friend of mine told me that once he was flirting with a woman and she said, "Let me rub your shoulders." He said, "Okay," and she grabbed him and started to aggressively dig in to his shoulders. He told me, "That was the end of the flirting, thank you very much." He got everything he needed to know. He did not want to be rammed through the wall.

People tell you a lot by the way they move their hands and what they do with them. Watch how they move their bodies. People who like their bodies move them differently from people who don't. When you hug people, notice the ones who ridge against you. Feel the ones that are unwilling to receive anything from you and those who try to give to you all the time. They push at you instead of inviting. Notice the ones who move in to you and receive you. That will begin to give you an indication of how to choose someone to be with. If there's no real receiving of you in a hug, they won't receive you in bed. People will let you know if they're interested in you. A lot of them will look at you and go, "Ooh, I want you." But then, they'll hug you and you'll know you don't want that.

If you're interested in a man, watch how he holds his wine glass. Does he stroke it? Then he'll stroke you. Notice how he hugs. If he forces energy at you, and he's not willing to melt together with you, he's not going to be good in bed. I've talked with a lot of women about their relationships with men, and I ask them, "What does your husband do?"

If they say, "He's a carpenter," I ask, "Does he treat you like a board? Does he hammer you?

Most of the time, they say, "Yes!"

Often, with carpenters, everything has to be at right angles. Everything is right or wrong, good or bad. It's not about the touching. If he does heavy-duty carpentry, chances are that's the way he's going to be with your body. You'll be another stick he has to nail. But when I ask women who are married to cabinetmakers if their husbands are sensual, they say, "Yes, he's very sensual." A cabinetmaker looks at the wood and feels the grain of it, and sees how it works. That's what you want—someone who works with and appreciates everything in nature.

WOULD YOU LIKE TO CREATE GREAT INTIMACY?

||||||||||||||||||||||||||||||||||||||||||||||||||||||||||||

The most extraordinary relationship I have ever seen was between Mary, a 94-year-old friend of mine, and her husband, Bill. I've never seen a couple care for each other more than those two people. The energy that flowed between them was beautiful.

Mary was raised in England by her Victorian grandmother and came to the United States in the early 1920s. She is remarkable in who she is, and has spent her whole life doing metaphysical research. Toward the end of his life, Bill had Alzheimer's. He got to the point where he couldn't remember anything and he would ask Mary the same questions over and over again, but she never got upset about this. She simply repeated the same answer or information as if she had never heard him ask the question before.

I learned about the five elements for creating great intimacy from Mary. She showed me how becoming intimate with your partner always begins by becoming intimate with yourself, and I watched as she continuously put these five elements—honor, trust, allowance, vulnerability, and gratitude—into practice in her relationship with Bill.

Honor

The first element for creating great intimacy is honor. As I said, this begins with honoring yourself. You have intimacy with yourself and you honor you. You don't divorce parts of yourself or deny or suppress them. You take care of yourself and do what is right for you. Then you must honor your partner. To honor your partner is to treat him or her with regard. You trust that the other person will take care of himself or herself and will do what is right for them, and you honor that, and at the same time, you do what is right for you.

Bill, for example, believed you lived once and you died and that was it. You became worm food. He couldn't have disagreed more with Mary's view of reincarnation, but he honored her viewpoint. And she did the same with him. They didn't argue about it, they didn't make one another wrong, and they didn't try to change the other. They allowed the other person to have their point of view totally.

If what honors you is to go out and ride a horse, and that's not what your partner does, but that's what you do, then you're honoring yourself if you ride. You don't dishonor your partner by expecting him to take up horseback riding. And he doesn't dishonor you, by getting upset that you aren't spending all of your time with him.

In my own relationship, my ex-wife spent money as fast as we could make it, and she often emptied out our bank accounts and bounced checks. This was difficult for me, because I would write checks to people that worked for me, only to find out they had bounced. Eventually I started to set money aside so I would have enough money to cover my employees' pay. I covered their bounced checks with the cash I had set aside and waited until there was money in the account and took it back.

There was no way in hell my ex-wife was going to change her financial behavior, no matter what I did, no matter what I said, no matter how much we talked about it. She couldn't change it. She didn't want to. She thought she did a great job of handling money. I could honor the fact that this was her way of doing things, and at the same time, I could honor myself by making sure I had enough money to cover my obligations. Setting money aside wasn't dishonoring her, even though she might have called it *dishonest*, because it didn't serve the desires she had.

Finally, I got to the point in this relationship where I saw I was divorcing myself continuously to make our marriage work. This is what most people do. They divorce themselves in order to create a relationship. This is what Mary and Bill did not do. Eventually I decided to end our marriage, and in doing so, I did my best to honor my ex-wife and to honor myself. I didn't say, "You've got to change these things I know you can't change." I said, "I realize that asking you to change these things would be like asking a leopard to change its spots. It's not going to happen, and it's dishonoring of you to ask that of you." I also honored myself. My viewpoint was, "Without these things changing, I can't live with you anymore."

I ensured that she got a substantial financial settlement. I wasn't trying to kill her off or do her damage. I wanted to honor the commitment I'd made to her by giving her a decent income for the next 10 or 15 years, because I'd promised I would do that. I wasn't trying to be mean, I wasn't trying to be ugly, I just couldn't live with her anymore. So, it was honoring of myself and honoring of her to handle the divorce in this way.

On the other side of this honoring your partner, there was a lady in one of my classes who decided than Dain was the perfect man for her. She called her husband and told him that Dain was interested in her and that he needed to change or she would go with Dain. Dain wasn't even offering that. She was operating from a place of, "My husband doesn't do what I want so I'm going to control him." She wasn't honoring herself, she wasn't honoring her husband, and she wasn't honoring Dain. When I asked her about what she had said to her husband, she said, "I told him that because I wanted to be honest with him."

I said, "That's not honest. That's mean. That's fucking cruel. What you did with that was to knife him. Why would you do that to someone you cared about? Even if you had decided you were going to leave him, telling him that would not be an honest or a kind thing to do." She was not treating him with regard.

Honoring yourself and your partner also applies to the area of so-called extra-marital affairs. When most people go off and have sex with someone besides their partner, it's *cheating*. It's not about honoring themselves, and it's certainly not about honoring their spouse. Occasionally, however, having sex with someone other than your partner can be about honoring yourself. We've worked with people who have told us stories about having sex with other people and how it changed their lives in truly beneficial ways. When that's the case, it has a different energy to it than *cheating*.

One man I worked with told me he had lived with his fiancée for a year and half and they had gotten to the point where they were having sex less than once a month, and he was starting to have problems with his body. He went away to a weekend event without his fiancée and met somebody there and they had sex. It opened up his universe and completely changed the way he thought about himself. He went, "Whoa, wait a minute, I'm not dead. I'm not undesirable. I'm not a jerk. I'm not an asshole. I'm not a bad person." He had sex with the woman only once, and then went home. The fact that this woman received him the way she did was hugely transforming for him.

This experience was deeply honoring to him, and it enabled him to become more intimate with himself. He found that as a result, he became more honoring of his fiancée. He didn't go home and tell her what he'd done. He just had the awareness for himself,

In such a circumstance, there's no need to go back and tell the other person because it's not about him or her. It's about what you needed to know and find out about you. It's not that you come away feeling guilty. You come away feeling more aware of yourself. You are more able to be present with your partner because you have stopped divorcing some piece of you.

Often when I begin to talk about this, people say things like, "If my husband ever cheated on me, I'd kill him!" I want you to understand that *cheating* is not honoring you, nor is it honoring your partner. If you're in a relationship and you go out and have sex with somebody else and you're doing it to prove, *I'm still sexy*, or *He wants me,* that is not honoring of you. You are actually dishonoring yourself.

If what you do is a transgression in your own eyes, then you have dishonored yourself, not to mention the other person. A transgression indicates you've done something wrong. But if you've been with someone other than your partner, and it's done from an honoring place, it will not have a detrimental effect. You aren't dishonoring your partner because you're not dishonoring you. That distinction needs to be made.

It's a much bigger point of view than the conventional one. If your partner has an affair with someone, is it really about you? Or is it about them? If they are doing it from a place of honoring themselves, it will not be something they did against you. If they need to do that for themselves, they should. And they shouldn't then tell you about it, because that would be dishonoring you.

Once when Mary and I were talking about this, I asked her, "Did Bill ever cheat on you?"

She said, "I have no idea. But if he needed to do that to honor himself, I trusted that he would do so.

I asked, "What about people who have affairs and go home and try to get their conscience clear by telling their partner?"

She said, "If you go home and put your dirty underwear over your partner's face and ask them to prove they love you anyway, you're really not being kind. You young people think you have to share your dirty laundry in order to have a relationship, but you are mistaken. That's not what honoring your partner is about."

Mary's view is that it is not honoring the other person to tell them what you think is bad about you, or what you think your transgression is. She said, "You don't degrade yourself in that way. You don't tell people things they cannot hear." She believed that truly honoring the other person is recognizing they don't need to be a part of that.

Trust

The second element for creating great intimacy is trust. You might think trust means blind faith. You're blind to everything that goes on. No. You don't want to be blind. You want to be aware. You trust that the person will always do what is best for them. You don't have blind faith that they're going to be faithful to you, that they're going to do what you want, or that they're going to deliver the goods. You're aware that they must always take care of themselves. Trust is simply knowing your partner is always going to do what he or she is going to do. As Mary put it, "I knew I could trust Bill to be who he was and to do what was right for him and that he would always honor me in whatever way he could."

You don't trust the other person to do what you *want* them to do. You trust them to do what they *will* do. If he's always going to leave the toilet seat up, then you trust him to do that. If she's always going to spend all the money on clothes, you trust her to do that.

People whose partners are alcoholics, for example, tend to *trust* that the alcoholic will change because they love them so much. They expect the alcoholic to become sober because of the relationship or the love they have. But you don't trust an alcoholic to stop drinking. If you do that, you're destroying your own awareness; you're making your decision about what you *want* greater than your awareness of what *is*. Trust is being aware that he's an alcoholic and knowing that as such, he's going to drink.

I know a woman whose view of her husband was, "He's wonderful. He's just fabulous. Now, if I could just get him to change!" But why would you marry someone you felt had to change? Do you like to buy fixer upper houses? Why do you choose fixer upper people? Wouldn't you rather move into a house and be happy with it the way it is? You don't have to settle for a dump to fix up. Take the house you get, and look and see what's great about it, and don't expect it to change. People expect their partners to change into what they want them to change into, rather than what they're actually going to change into. And then they get angry, because they *trusted* that person would change. That's not trust. Trust is, *This person is never going to be any different than they are—unless they choose to be.*

Trust that if you get into a relationship with someone who was *cheating* on his wife, he'll probably be cheating on you, too. Trust that. If she cheated on her former husband and then she went with you, she's going to do it again. Trust that the leopard is a leopard. It's not a kitty-cat now. And decide from there whether that's the person you want in your life.

Years ago when I had roommates, people would apply to be my new roommate and they'd look at the house, which was always very tidy, and they'd say, "I'm a really clean person." That was always a lie. People will tell you what they think you need to hear. They would say, "Oh, I share my food," which meant they would eat my food and be upset if I ate anything of theirs.

I had one roommate who never mentioned that he was clean, never mentioned he was tidy, never mentioned he shared his food, and he was the best roommate I ever had. He was easy to be around. He contributed to everything. You can trust that when somebody says they are this or that, they are probably not. Just know that. And honor yourself with not cutting off your awareness and trying to make a lie into a truth.

Allowance

Allowance is the third element for creating great intimacy. Allowance is the attitude that everything that goes on is just an interesting point of view. When you're in allowance, thoughts, ideas, beliefs, attitudes, and emotions come at you, and they go around you, and you're still you. You don't buy the idea that the things the other person is talking about have to affect you—it's just their point of view. You don't have to resist or react to what they say or do and you don't have to agree or align with it. When you're in allowance, you're in awareness and you don't have to do anything at all. You simply allow them to have their point of view—you are in allowance of what they're doing and how they're doing it. You allow them to be everything they are without expecting anything of them.

When you are in allowance with each other, you will not criticize. Criticism is based on, *I want you to do it my way.* That's not allowance. That's looking for alignment and agreement, which lead to resistance and reaction. When you don't align and agree with your partner's point of view, you'll stop trying to make the other person your whole life, and when you no longer resist and react, you won't have arguments. Don't try to stop your partner from being different than you are. Have a life. Let your partner have a life.

Mary and Bill were a great example of this. I mentioned that Mary devoted her life to a study of metaphysics. Bill was not the slightest bit interested in the subject, and he even thought what Mary was doing was weird. But his attitude was, "If that's what you want to do, go do it." He never stopped her, even when she was away from home for long periods of time, taking classes. He never objected to the money she spent on it. He didn't believe the same things she did, but he wanted her to have her life.

I asked Mary, "How long did you study metaphysics in England?"

"Three months," she replied.

"Did you and Bill call each other all the time?"

"Never. We just wrote letters."

"Well, when Bill went away on business trips, did you call each other?"

"No, he would call me the night before he got home to find out whether I was going to pick him up at the train, or whether he should take a taxi."

What! When I was married, my wife called me three times a day when I was working. She wanted to make sure I was under her control.

The only thing Bill asked of Mary around her metaphysical studies is that she didn't discuss them with his clients. No big deal, right? And she said, "Of course."

Don't buy the idea that the things your partner is talking about have to affect you. What they say is their point of view—it's not who they are. Who they are is who you married. Just be in allowance of what they are doing and how they're doing it. Allow them to be everything they are without expecting anything of them.

Vulnerability

The fourth element for creating great intimacy is vulnerability. Vulnerability means being an open wound. There's no scab on it, there's no bandage over it, there's just total sensitivity, which means you receive all the information. Have you ever had a stubbed toe? Have you noticed that everyone seems to step on it? You're so aware of it, that you keep sticking it out there even when you're trying not to.

Mary told me, "You have to be totally vulnerable with the other person. No barriers. You have to just be there, present." Everything is possible. You receive everything they have and you keep your barriers down.

If your partner comes at you with anger, stand there and let the anger go through you. You'll find that he or she will run out of steam in about three minutes. If you don't put up a barrier, people have nothing to bang against and they don't have to exert force trying to make themselves right.

If you wish to create an extraordinary relationship, you have to notice when the automatic barriers go up and learn to keep them down. Force the barriers down, and anything the other person does or says is neither right nor wrong, good nor bad; it's just an interesting point of view.

What does this look like in real life? My ex-wife is a person who grew up with anger as a power source, so whenever she got upset about something, she'd start delivering anger at me. When she did this all my shields would go up. I'd stand there with my shields up and she'd beat on them until I either dropped them or ran away.

After I learned about vulnerability I said, "Okay, I've got to be vulnerable no matter what," and I started forcing the barriers down. If you wish to create an extraordinary relationship, you have to see where you put up the automatic barriers and start forcing them down. Somebody who is angry wants someone to slam. They want something to beat. If you take away what they can beat at, they go, "Uh, never mind," and it creates a whole different reality. You force the barriers down and you let the other person deliver whatever it is, with the attitude that it's just their point of view at the moment.

In a very short period of time the anger will dissipate. When I pushed my barriers down, my ex would run out of steam within minutes. If I kept the barriers up, she could go on for hours. Know that if you have somebody who goes on and on at you, it's because you're keeping your barriers up. Lower them—shove them out of the way and the other person will run out of steam. They cannot continue to deliver force at you if there's no place for the force to bump against, so it flows back at them and lets them know they're getting a result. If it just goes on through, you're totally vulnerable.

As long as the other person is in anger, they're going to force energy at you and they're not going to truly be present. When you push your barriers down you can start to have a sense of connection and communication with the person. You let the barriers down and once they run out of steam, you can actually be present for them and have a communication about the subject. True communication cannot occur as long as you are doing barriers.

Anger is one of the more intense situations that will tend to activate your barriers, and if you can remain vulnerable and keep your barriers down in the face of anger, you're doing well. There are many other situations and areas in our lives where we put up barriers and they range from the glaringly obvious to the subtle.

Barriers are actually defense systems people use to fend off real communication. Some people use their intellect as a barrier.

They say, "You don't know as much as I do." Other people use their emotions as a barrier. They create huge emotional tirades with trauma and drama, and say, "You don't understand me!" And some people use no sex as a barrier. No sex is, "Keep out. You can't come here. I am not having sex with you. I'm not willing to receive any part of you."

Recognize that when you put up one of these barriers, you are blocking the other person from being present with you. You're in your own little world. It's a way of controlling everything, because there is no solution to be found for the barrier that you're putting up. The sole purpose of it is to create separation between you and them so you don't have communion and you don't have intimacy.

Although it might feel counter-intuitive to you at the time, you just feel the barrier and you say, "This is going down. I'm not putting this up." You're willing to fight a limitation that you hide behind. You are willing to fight for yourself and your relationship by forcing the barriers out of existence.

Just recognize it when the barriers start coming up, "Oh, I'm putting my barriers up," and shove the damn things down. Be conscious enough to know it's a barrier and get it down. The truth is, if you are totally vulnerable, no one will ever hurt you.

Gratitude

The final element for creating great intimacy is gratitude. Mary said, "You have to have gratitude." It's not love you want. It's gratitude. Most of you would call it unconditional love, but the reality is that if you have the point of view of unconditional love, then you also have the other side of it, the attitude of conditional love, which means you will put a judgment on it. With unconditional love, you have to judge whether or not it's something you can be unconditional about. You're still sitting in judgment, but with gratitude you cannot judge.

You're grateful for who the other person is. You're caring and loving and nurturing of their body and they return that to you. But it's not about the return. It's about the gift you receive when you have that point of view.

You're grateful for that body being next to you because it's warm, it's cuddly, it's fuzzy, and it's got parts you can hold onto. In working with couples, I have found that many times men and women do not really care for the body of the other sex. They're not enchanted with it, they don't think it's wonderful. Their partner's body is something they use for sex rather than something they find beautiful and want to caress and look at fondly. If you can look at the other person's body and think, "Oh, how beautiful!" the body begins to react and put forth more sexual energy.

Start developing your gratitude. What are you grateful for about the person you're with? In that gratitude for them, you expand your reality and theirs. That will lead you into sexualness, which can include copulation. Unless you have gratitude, the copulation is not going to be as great as you'd like it to be.

Allowance, Trust, Honor, Vulnerability and Gratitude for *Yourself*

Because, as Mary said, becoming intimate with a partner always begins by becoming intimate with yourself, you must begin to develop the five elements of great intimacy with yourself. Until you can have allowance with yourself and for yourself, and trust yourself, and honor yourself, be vulnerable with yourself, and have gratitude for who you are and whatever you create in your life, you can't have anybody else in your life. You'll always be looking for someone to validate your beingness. *He makes me happy.* No. There's only one person who can make you happy. You.

Relationship, by definition, is the distance or the separation between two objects. If I'm in relationship with you, that means I'm not you. *Relationship* takes away the possibility of oneness and creates a perpetual separation. People go into their relationships thinking, "Oh, they're this —and I'm this." And then they begin divorcing parts and pieces of themselves to make them okay in the relationship. "Oh, I don't want to do this, because then they won't like me." They start to change themselves.

A person falls in love with you. They see, for ten seconds, the amazing being you truly are, and they go, "That's the person I want to be with."

Then you have a judgment about yourself. You go, "Oh, I can't let them see this part of me, because this is bad." You divorce a piece of who you are, so you don't show up.

And then, pretty soon, they're divorcing parts of themselves. The two of you have divorced so much of who you were in the beginning that you have nothing in common anymore. Pretty soon you have two strangers living together.

But the reality is, that for those ten seconds, the other person saw all of you; the good, the bad, and the ugly, and they saw it all without judgment. If you would allow yourself to be all of who you are, at all times, and not divorce yourself, then you could have a truly extraordinary relationship.

If you practice the five elements to great intimacy, you won't divorce yourself. You won't stop being you in the relationship. How much of you did you divorce in your last relationship? Most people say about 150,000 percent of themselves. Hardly anyone says less than 90 percent. You divorce 90 percent of you to create a relationship? Where are *you* in the relationship? And who are you in relationship with? And by the way, when did you leave the relationship?

I was working with a lady who was whining, "Oh, my husband left me and I'm so devastated. My life sucks and nothing is working."

I said, "Really? When did you leave the relationship? Three months before you got married or three months after?"

She started to laugh. "Three months before! I knew it wasn't going to work. I knew it wasn't going to be a good relationship."

"And how long did you stay with him?" I asked.

"Ten years," she said.

"Good idea! And why did you not end the relationship when you knew it wouldn't work?

"Because," she said, "The wedding invitations were already printed and the caterer was hired and the venue was paid for."

"And you wouldn't waste $1000 to not have 10 years of pain and suffering for what reason? I'm sorry. I think you're a little insane in this area."

I see people do this all the time. How much of you do you divorce to create a relationship? If you have to divorce any part of you, get out! If your partner cannot be in allowance of exactly who you are and if you cannot do what you need to do, and what's good for you, go away, because you don't want to be with them, and you aren't with them. And they aren't with you. Move on. There are billions of fish in the sea. Just because you have one of them on the hook doesn't mean you have to eat it, in the good way or the bad way.

If having a relationship with someone expands your existence, then go for it. If it becomes a contraction of your life, you're dying. It's not a good deal. That is not what communion is. True communion allows each of you to expand. You never have to give up part of you for the other person, because he or she will have total gratitude for you, for exactly who you are, and would never ask you to change in order to be with him or her.

With the five elements for creating intimacy, you can eliminate *relationship,* the separation between you, and create a *communion* that is a constant state of expansiveness.

FOR MEN:

YOU WANT TO SEDUCE A WOMAN?

||||||||||||||||||||||||||||||||||||||||

You want to seduce a woman? Well, invite her to your house. Cook her a great dinner. Have candlelight, china, and good crystal. Put on nice music and ask her questions about herself all night long and never tell her anything about yourself. At the end of the evening, say, "Would you like me to take you home or would you like to spend the night with me?" She'll say, "You know, you're the most interesting man I've ever met. I'd love to spend the night with you."

Want to get a woman interested? Listen. Ask her lots of questions about her day, what she did and how she's feeling. Ask what would feel pleasurable to her, what she would like.

And while you're doing it, pull massive amounts of energy from her, because she wants to feel attracted to you. When you start pulling massive amounts of energy through every pore of your body and your being, she'll look at you and think, "He's such an attractive man."

And on top of that, you're listening. You have just seduced her totally. If you listen without any judgment, you'll get laid every time. I guarantee it. But you've got to pull massive amounts of energy— that's how you do it. Usually what happens when you start to get horny is that you flow energy at women. That doesn't work because they go, "Ew, that feels yucky." But if you pull energy from them, they go, "Oh, he's so wonderful, he's so attractive. I can't keep my hands off him."

Have you ever had one of those days when you're feeling really good, you're strutting your stuff, you're walking tall and you've got a great outfit on and everybody's looking at you? They're stopping on the street and smiling at you? It's not that you're wearing nice clothes or that you're feeling good that day. No. It's that you're actually pulling energy. You're pulling energy from all over the universe and allowing it to come in to you. You are totally willing to receive at that moment, and everybody wants to come into your space.

Do you want to see Madonna at her sexiest? Watch her in *Dick Tracy*, where she doesn't move a muscle. The one thing Madonna has working for her, is that she pulls energy—she can suck the chrome of a '58 Buick at 500 yards, by the energy she pulls. She sucks you right in. That's the difference between somebody who thinks well of herself and pulls energy—and someone who doesn't.

It just takes practice, but you have to be conscious enough to know that's what it takes to get what you're looking for. You have to be attractive and the only way people will consider you attractive is if you pull energy from them. You just ask the energy to pull. Practice it by going into Starbucks and pulling energy from everybody in the place until they all turn around and look at you. The caveat is you have to be willing to be seen as you.

Can you have sex if you aren't willing to receive? No, you can't. You can only have sex when you're willing to receive. When you push energy at somebody, it pushes them away. This is why all the women you're not interested in come to you. The easiest way in the world to make someone that's not interested in you interested is to pull energy like crazy and appear as though you're not interested in them.

That's what women do with guys. It's why guys go ga-ga over women. The woman they find attractive is the one that's pulling energy from them. What guys tend to do is force energy at the woman, thinking, "She's pulling energy. She must want me to force energy at her." When you do that, every woman in the world goes, "Yuck, I hate that guy!" When you flow massive amounts of energy, that's the result you create. When you do that, the sex you have is not a receiving or a gifting. It's the force and violence that pornography is, and most women don't like pornography.

If you know that the women who are attractive to you are pulling energy, then you have a reference point for what it feels like, and you can do it, too.

WHERE IS THE ENERGY? FIND IT BEFORE YOU MAKE LOVE
||||||||||||||||||||||||||||||||||||

Sexualness comes from the being that you are. It's not about the body; it's about who you are and what you have inside. Copulation, on the other hand, comes from the body. If you're going to enjoy great copulation, you have to turn her body on to get things going. You want to find the energy before you make love. Where is it? What creates sexual energy?

One of the most sensitive places on any person's body is their feet. If you want to start sex, a great way to begin is by giving her a foot massage, which will relax her and get her into communication with her body. Start between the big toe and the second and third toes and rub diligently but gently on the top and bottom of the foot at the same time. Then, gradually move to the pressure points behind the heels, and that will start to turn her body on.

Then ask her to turn face down, and start at the bottom of her feet. Touch her with just the back of your fingertips and run them up her legs and then up her body, and stroke her so lightly that you're almost not even touching her. Start to blow up between her legs and up to the top of her buttocks and move up her body and rub her head a little bit.

Don't do it from the point of view, *Okay, I'm going to get laid,* because that kills the energy. Do it from the point of view of, *What does her body want?* Massage wherever her body tells you to. When you touch in different places, ask the body, "Where would you like to be touched and what kind of touch would you like to have?" You're gifting to the body. Most people step out of their bodies during sex. They just leave their bodies and go away, but if you do this very light gentle touch on a woman, you're inviting her to stay present in her body rather than stepping out. You'll turn her body on by asking it where it wants to be touched and how it wants to be gifted to, and the end result will be far more dynamic than anything you have experienced before.

While you're stroking her, smell the different parts of her body, because the ankles and the calves and the thighs and the crotch all smell differently. The back of the buttocks has its own scent. Every place has a different perfume. It's not the perfume she puts on; it's the perfume of her body, what people call pheromones. When you do those things, you are being sensual and they will start to turn you on, as well.

If you use all the sensations of the body as a way of turning yourself on, you'll turn her on, too. And as your body starts to get hard, as it starts to get excited, the sexual energy of your body will turn her body on even more. That starts to prepare the process.

Have her turn over again, and ask the body where it wants to be touched and do the same light touch. Ignore the crotch until the last possible minute. I know that's hard, but you have to ignore it. The longer you ignore it, the hotter she's going to be and the more willing she's going to be to do anything you want.

Armpits are seduction spots. Ear lobes, interior of the ears, behind the ears, the neck, just touch them. Don't do the kissing and making out routine because that's what she expects you to do and then she knows she has control. When you do what I am suggesting, her body loses control and starts to demand of her that she has sex.

When she gets to the point where she can hardly stand it and she wants you to caress her, go lightly over her crotch, just lightly touch the hairs. Don't get in and dig or any of that, just lightly stroke her and when she starts to moan and groan and writhe a little bit, you can start to massage that area lightly.

Don't rush it. You want to get to the point where your sexual energy is up so much that her body becomes sexually aroused as well. It becomes a communion and a cohesion of the two bodies working together. That's what you're looking for. The bodies work together and start to facilitate each other in an orgasmic experience. It's not about the force. It's about the infinite intensity and lightness of energy. You want more intensity, less force. The less force you use, the more intense and expansive, you make it.

You will want to be able to recognize when your partner starts to go away. You can gently ask her, "Okay, so where did you just go?" You want to keep her present because if she's present, she'll enjoy sex and she'll enjoy you. Ultimately you'll get to the point where you can have sex with a woman and feel everything her body is feeling and everything your body is feeling. You'll experience everything your body is doing for her body, and everything her body is doing for your body. That is total communion, a total awareness of both bodies sharing the connection and communion, this intensity of infiniteness.

You know the clitoris is the most sensitive part of a woman's body. So make your tongue like a butterfly wing and use it over her clit until it starts to rise up to you. Suck a little bit and use more tongue action and put your finger in her vagina. Ask her body to show you where the most sensitive spot is and gently rub it. Just about the time when she's just about to hit it, when she's getting really intense, stop and start to lick very slowly up and down and make it so slow that she starts to vibrate. Do that at the same time as you are rubbing your finger inside her vagina and you should be able to get her to the point where she will have anywhere from seven to 15 orgasms in about an hour and a half.

When she can't take it any longer and demands that you come in, don't do it even then. Hold it off until it is so intense that she can't stand it. It will be sex like you've never had it before. Grab the pubic hairs and just pull a little bit. If you can touch the nipples and tweak them lightly so they become hard, that will involve the whole body in the process, not just the genitals.

You do all of this while following the energy. You've got to follow the energy because you want to invite her body to orgasm. You don't force it. Most people try to force orgasm by getting more intense, with more action and friction. You want to have more energy and less pressure. Less pressure, more invitation.

Once you have had a little sex, get your penis very stiff, keep it in her and just barely move. Increase the intensity of the energy of almost no movement to the point where she starts to violently come against you with your penis inside her.

Then, if you're up for it and she is, you can pull it out and do anal sex. All of your judgments about anal sex, can we destroy and un-create those please?

While you are having sex, if you will make the feelings you are having infinite and draw the person you are having sex with into that infiniteness, it becomes an intensity that is quite extraordinary.

The Largest Organ in Your Body Is Your Skin

Our bodies are actually incredible sensual organs. They like sensations and they love to be touched. Use your whole body to have sex, not just your penis. The largest organ in your body is your skin. Feel the sensations of all of it and start to develop your capacity to be totally sensate in every inch of your skin.

When you masturbate, do you touch your whole body or do you just touch your penis? Start to use your whole body when you masturbate, and make masturbation something that's intense, not by the speed of it, but by its slowness. This will start to develop in your body the sense of being caressed and invited to orgasm, rather than being forced into it. You will develop the capacity to have the slowness and the intensity of that orgasmic energy available to you.

If you have hair on your body, do you use it as a caressing thing? Do you move your body like a snake over your partner's body or do you tend to go bam- bam-bam thank you ma'am? The more you can move with her body, the more you can feel the different parts of her body, her full body, the same thing will happen for you that happens for her.

Ask her body what it would like and in gifting her that, her body will try to return the favor to you because it will be grateful to your body. Bodies love other bodies. They take care of them if you allow them to.

FOR WOMEN:

YOU HAVE TOTAL CONTROL
||||||||||||||||||||||||||||||||||||||||||||||||||||||||||||||||||||||||||||||||||

One of the things I would like you to recognize is that women have total control over everything that happens in sex. If you don't know that and haven't claimed and owned it, you'd better start looking at it, because men come when you ask. They can pant all they want, but unless you choose them, they don't get you. Ever notice that? Stop pretending that you're weak, pale and don't get what you want because you always get what you want if you go after it.

He might try to come after you but it's always your choice whether you take him or not. A man will always choose sex. A woman makes the choice about whether she has sex or not.

WOULD YOU LIKE TO GIVE HIM A FULL BODY ORGASM?

||||||||||||||||||||||||||||||||||||||||||||||||||||||||||||||||||||||||||||||||

Have him lay him face down on the bed, and start massaging his feet. You want to create a connection between his body and him, because most people aren't present during sex. You want to get him so present that he'll start to scream for orgasm.

Tell him that he's not to move and he's not to touch you. His job is to just receive, and you want to gift him something he's never had before. Begin by massaging his feet, especially in between the big toe and the second toe and up the foot into the arch. This will start to pull him into his body and get him connected. It also starts to open up the channels that allow energy to go up the whole body.

Then, while he's still lying face down, take your fingernails and begin to stroke his body very lightly, as gently as you can, so that the hair on his body stands up and reaches for your hand.

While you're doing this, smell his ankles, smell the backs of his knees, because there are different odors in each of those places. Each one of those scents is a pheromone that is designed to turn on your body, so you'll start to turn your body on, as well as his, and you'll both become more present. Move your hands up and gently massage his buttocks. If you feel like it, lick the crack of his buttocks. Continue up to the small of this back and kiss it gently. Move up, very gently, to his shoulders and down his arms. Lightly tickle inside his hands. Then run your hands up his neck and through his hair to get him connected to all of his body.

Ask him if he'd like to turn over. If he does, and he has an erection, tell him, "Okay now, just be still. Don't do anything now. Don't touch. You can't touch. You have to receive."

Start at his feet once again and lightly stroke his feet and his calves and his thighs. Gently move your fingers over his penis and his testicles, stroking him so lightly that you are barely touching him at all. Continue to move up his body lightly stroking the front of him, his face and his ears, the top of his head.

Then, with the same light touch, slowly move down from the top of his head to his penis. If he's not hard by that time, even if he's soft, put his penis in your mouth and very gently massage it like it's the most delicate, wonderful thing you've ever experienced in your life.

As he starts to get harder, make your touch lighter and lighter and lighter. Put your mouth over his penis and run your tongue up the penis, very lightly and gently, keep rubbing it up and down like a snake going across the top of the penis. Then put your lips around the base of the penis as far down as you can get, and start to pull in and suck up a little bit and use the inside of your upper teeth, lightly, lightly, on the underside of his penis so it creates a little bit of a friction. Or if you can do it more easily with the inside of your mouth or your gums, do that. Ask his body what it wants.

If you feel like it, you can take the scrotum and suck it into your mouth, or you can suck his testicles. Let his body tell you what to do. The idea here is to gift and receive. You are gifting to him—and in so doing, you are receiving simultaneously.

Before you start, make sure you have next to you on the bed a good anal lubricant, something that's thick and will give lots of lubrication. Put some of the lubricant on your middle finger or two fingers. Most men haven't had their anus played with so they're a little tight and they can't handle two fingers to start with. Put a lot of lubricant on your middle finger and start to rub around his anus. Stick your finger inside and start to rub. The prostate is toward the upper side of the body. Begin to rub that area. It's not so much the in and out, it's about rubbing that area. If you can get two fingers in there, rub the two fingers back and forth as though you're trying to tickle something and keep doing the blowjob. A lot of times when men have not had anal stimulation, they will lose their erection, but no matter, just keep squishing his penis in your mouth and be as gentle as possible. As you do that, pull the energy.

You want him to be totally present. If you feel he is not being present, put your hand up on his chest and push energy there and he'll start pulling into his body, so he can actually be there. Keep going on, as lightly as possible. As you rub, the prostate will start to get hard and just before he ejaculates, it will get like two little testicles that are hard as rocks. When he gets to that point, keep rubbing and go more slowly on the blowjob until finally he explodes.

When the explosion comes, begin to vibrate your fingers against the prostate. Put your hand on his chest and vibrate the energy up his whole body. Within the first few times of doing this about seventy percent of men will have a full body orgasm. He'll start to vibrate and go out of his head and you'll never, ever be able to get rid of him again.

The most important thing is to do it very gently and slowly. It's not the friction. Most men, when they masturbate, use friction and speed. That's not what you want to do. You want to invite his body to orgasm. Use less pressure to create a greater intensity of energy. It's about the energy you're creating, not the amount of pressure you are using.

Once you have gifted him with a full body orgasm, he'll be yours forever. Make sure you want to own him before you do it.

MOST MEN ARE NOT ABLE TO RECEIVE

||||||||||||||||||||||||||||||||||||||||||||||||||||||||

For most men, sex has never been about receiving, it has always been about giving or doing. It is imperative, when you are giving him a full body orgasm, to realize that you are gifting this man with something he has never received before. In fact, he's probably never been received sexually in his whole life. You want to create a communion with him and his body, and gift to him by letting him receive. It's not been done.

Women, for the most part, have never learned how to gift. For them, sex has been about how they have to receive and the point of view has been that women are the receiving end of things and men are the plug in. I'm sorry, but you are not male and female electrical sockets. Get over that point of view.

You have to give in to the idea of gifting and receiving and the simultaneity of it. Truly, that's how it can be if you're willing to be totally present, and if they are.

It's important for women to know that men never receive, and that they don't know how. They've never been taught. Usually, a man's point of view is, "I'm ready to have you," which is not receiving. If you think about it, one reason a whole lot of men only know how to do sexualness as force and friction and violence is because they watch porn flicks. That's the only place they see men having sex, and there's certainly no receiving or gifting going on in a porn flick.

Men are not taught to be sensual. A woman is expected to be sensual, but most of the time, she doesn't know how to do that, either. The truth is, usually she doesn't know how to receive any better than a man does. She just thinks she does. Of all the women Dain and I have known, there have been very few who could truly receive sexually. It is a great sadness to us that more people don't know how to enjoy their bodies and experience the greatness and the possibilities that can occur when they are able to be truly present, and not divorce themselves, in order to have sex.

What would it be like if you could have great copulation, amazing communion, and the infinite possibilities of a relationship that is totally expansive and joyful? What would it be like to have a relationship that deals with the issues of life, and doesn't become bogged in them? To have a relationship that expands your life, instead of killing it or contracting it? What would it be like to create your life rather than existing it or living from the obligation of it? This is what we wish for you to achieve. Awareness is the beginning.

And remember: *Practice makes perfect!*

A NOTE TO READERS
||||||||||||||||||||||||||||||||||||||||||||||||||||||||||||||||||

Access is an energy transformation program which links seasoned wisdom, ancient knowledge and channeled energies with highly contemporary motivational tools. Its purpose is to set you free by giving you access to your truest, highest self.

The information, tools and techniques presented in this book are just a small taste of what Access has to offer. There is a whole universe of Access processes and classes.

If there are places where you can't get things in your life to work the way you know they ought to, you might be interested in attending an Access class or workshop or locating an Access facilitator, who can work with you to give you greater clarity about issues you can't overcome. Access processes are done with a trained facilitator, and are based on the energy of you and the person you're working with.

For more information, visit www.accessraz.com or www. accessbeing.com

CPSIA information can be obtained at www.ICGtesting.com
Printed in the USA
LVOW042056190612

286827LV00002B/203/A